The Layla Diaries

Dr. Layla
OPEN FOR
BUSINESS

Sonya Bartlett Skipworth

thelayladiaries@yahoo.com

ISBN:0998474703
ISBN-13:9780998474700

DEDICATION

To Ben and Sarah—I am so thankful to be your Mom

and

To Phillip, "G"—You still give me butterflies . . .

ACKNOWLEDGMENTS

Photographic credits:
Front Cover—Jessie B. Skipworth, Inkwell Films
Back Cover—Ben Skipworth, Inkwell Films

Editorial Services:
Brenda J. Burns

DISCLAIMER

Excuse me. May I please have your attention? The information in this book is not intended to treat or diagnose any medical condition. You should consult a veterinarian if you think your pet needs medical attention.

I don't know why but my Grammy told me to say those words. It must mean, "Layla is just a pup. What does she know anyway?"

Dr. Layla
Nashville, Tennessee

Introduction

Hellos! I still live in Nashville, Tennessee with my Mom and Dad. I still get to visit my Grammy and G in Alabama. I still have adventures. Since I became Dr. Layla, I have been getting flea-mails from other pups from all over the place asking for advice. It is a glad thing in my heart when I can help someone else—especially a fellow fur friend.

When they sent me their letters I loved reading them very much. I enjoyed looking at their pictures because it helped me decide how to answer. I hope you will like their letters and my answers. I'm going to ask G for some ice cream now. Maybe he will say yes. Who am I kidding? It's G! Of course he will say "Yes!"

Hello Dr. Layla,

My name is York. York the bully, to be exact. I am a 10 month old English bulldog who is known for great pick-up lines and for my ridiculously good looks. I have a lovely family. However, there are some things I don't understand about my parents and I'm hoping you have those answers.

Every time I'm on the couch, the pillows are ready to attack my humans. But I don't get fooled by their fluffiness. So, I eat the pillows until all their fluff is gone. Why do my parents get mad? I just saved their life!

I love food. I get special organic food in my personal bowl, but sometimes I just want my mom and dad's food. So I sit on the table to make sure my parents see me. It never ends up good. I am immediately put into puppy time out. Why is that? When did sitting on the table become such a bad thing?

In the mornings sometimes I like to leave brown, scented gifts for my parents. I want them to know I appreciate them. They wake up to gifts a lot! I think it is a special surprise. But my parents don't see it that way! How can I show them it's my way of saying thank you?

Love,
York, the bully

"York the Bully"
I am loved by Anya

Dearest York the Bully,

I think you are a handsome fellow. I am sure all the girls in your area think so too! I'm not certain as to why parents have such a problem with the pillow fluffs since they can be so vicious! You never know when a pillow is going to hop off the couch and injure someone, so I agree you must be on guard to take care of all your peoples.

To address your second problem: I think moms and dads do not understand that we want to eat at the table like them. My Mom and Dad have lots of peoples to come over to our house. I have never seen them put their plate on the floor and make them eat away from the table. Sometimes they just don't get it that we just want to be included. Don't take it personal, York. They don't know any better.

I leave my Mom and Dad doodles too. I've never figured out why they don't leave one for me though. Maybe you could try leaving them a few more. Then they might get the hint. One morning you just might wake up and your mom or your dad will have left you a doodle in the floor as a surprise. I think that might make my Dad gag but I'm sure it would be an interesting start for the day.

Love,
Dr. Layla

Hello fur girly!

My name is Sampson, and I am a fur boy. I will be fourteen tomorrow! That's right, fourteen toes! That's almost four...SQUIRREL...what was I saying? Oh yeah, that's almost four paws! I was born in South Carolina, and now live at Double Head in Town Creek. I like it better here because there are more fish and squirrels.....SQUIRREL!

I've got a big family to take care of, but I love them. My question for you is how do you drink out of the toilet without mom noticing? You would think I would have learned over the years how to sneak a sip, but nope!

Thanks Layla, and I hope to sniff you soon!
Sampson

"Sampson"
I am loved by Jim, Sonya,
Weston, Sam, and Anna

Dear Sampson,

You have asked a very good question. My Mom will not let me drink out of the bathroom water fountain either. It is so convenient but my Mom gets upset if I try to do it. I'm saving her the trouble of not having to fill my water bowl so often. She doesn't agree.

I think I have a sneaky idea, if you are willing to try it. Maybe if you used a straw she would not hear you lapping up the water. I think, if I were you, I would try that and see if works.

Love,
Dr. Layla

5

Dearest Layla,

My name is Clooney! I'm a mutt, which means I'm part this and part that...but Mommy says all that means is that I'm 100% cute! I like to let my Mom and Dad give me belly rubs as often as possible...it makes them feel important. I am extremely regal and take my job as Prince Clooney very seriously!

Whenever I do take my weekly nap, it's either on Mom's lap or the fluffiest bunch of pillows I can find. My favorite food is peanut butter, closely followed by bacon. No, make that bacon followed by peanut butter. Wait, definitely....both. My breath may be stinky sometimes, but nobody remembers that when they're laughing hysterically at me chasing my tail.

I love to explore the wonderful and weird streets of Austin, Texas with my Mom and Dad. What I would do all day, if I could, is run and play outside! I run at least 200 mph. My favorite thing is to be chased...sometimes I bite other dog's tails, nibble their ears, and play tug-o-war with their toys all so they'll chase me so I can feel that glorious breeze on my face.

But, there's this one friend -- he's an acrobatic guy with a bit of a hoarding problem and a bushy tail. He just doesn't get my game. Every time I want to play with him, he gets scared and flees. What's worse is that I can't catch him because he climbs so high into the trees! I yell and yell and yell for him to come down and play, but he just stares blankly at me. How can I get him to play chase with me?

Sincerely,
CloonDog

Clooney
I am loved by Lyle and Emily

Hellos Clooney!

I was very happy to get your letter. My Grammy said your friend with the bushy tail is called a squirrel. When my Dad was a kid, some men were cutting a tree down in front of G's office. My Dad found a baby squirrel. It did not have a mom. Now that is a sad thing in my heart.

Grammy told my Dad he could not keep it. She said it was too little and wouldn't like living inside their house. My Dad did not listen to Grammy. He smuggled it home and hid it in his room. He gave the squirrel the name of Stewie. He and my Aunt Sarah took it to school with them every day in an ice cream bucket and fed him with a bottle.

One night my Grammy was walking down the hall and my Dad came out of the bathroom with the dish washing soap and Grammy asked him what he was doing. He tried to make up a good story and suddenly "Stewie" popped out from under his shirt. Grammy was not a happy lady.

My Dad started saying how Stewie didn't have a squirrel mom and my Grammy felt bad in her heart and let the little guy stay. My Dad built Stewie a small house in his bedroom.

Grammy was right about Stewie. He was too young to be without his mom. After a while he went over the Rainbow Bridge and my Dad was very, very sad. I wish I had been there then because I would have kissed his face and made him feel better.

So, if you tell Mr. Bushy Tail the story about my Dad and Stewie he might think it is OK to play with you. And maybe don't yell at him. I think that is not a good way to make friends.

Yours Truly,
Dr. Layla

Dear Layla

I am an Aussie too, except I am a Blue Merle. I live in Gilbert, Arizona. I had a birthday in June and I am seven! I love to talk...err...I mean bark. My humans keep telling me "quiet" "enough" "no".... and really all I hear is them telling me to bark LOUDER. Can you pleassse help them figure out how to really teach me to not bark all the time?

XOXO,
Izak

"Izak"
I am loved by Ashley

Hellos Izak!

I can relate to your problem. I hear a lot of "No barking Layla. Be quiet Layla. Stop whining Layla." My peoples talk to me all the time and say things like, "What do you think Layla?" Then when I am actually thinking of something I want to tell them they say, "Layla, stop barking!" Make up your mind peoples! Do you want to know what is on Layla's mind or not?

I'm not sure why they don't want me to talk. They are always looking at me and asking, "Layla, do you need to go out?" I just look at my Mom and say. "Yes, that is why I am doing the potty dance. I need to go out!" Somehow she understands that so I don't get why she can't always figure out what I'm trying to tell her.

She needs to be aware when Mr. Cat is lurking outside the window. I also need to warn her that there are squirrels in the yard. I feel it is my responsibility to tell her there are leaves blowing on the sidewalk. I don't want her to miss anything!

I'm thinking maybe you should just keep repeating yourself and say the same thing over and over. When peoples can't hear they say, "What?" Then the other peoples say it again. Just keep saying it until they figure it out. And, say it really, really loud.

Love,
Dr. Layla

Hello Layla!

Given that I am a German Shepherd, it is in my nature to hunt. My father and mother hate when I hunt for rabbits. One time, I brought one back to my mother and she cried. I'm only protecting them from the evil bunnies. Why will they not allow me to be myself?

Your bestie,
Wendy

Wendy
I am loved by Ben, Natalie, and Max

Hellos Wendy!

Your Mom loves rabbits? My peoples love rabbits too! Grammy has a gray one that lives near her house. She is always stopping her car to watch it bounce back into the woods. Maybe your mom just likes to watch them like Grammy. I don't know why because they are not exciting at all. They just sit and wiggle their noses. But I do know they are fast runners.

You might want to consider another kind of gift for your mom. I'm pretty sure she would not like to have a chewed up rabbit as a present. Moms usually think stuff like that is kind of gross.

My Dad had a rabbit before I was bornded. His name was Chunk. I guess he was kind of chubby. My Dad won him at the fair. At least that's what he told Grammy. When My Dad moved to Nashville he had to let Chunk live with a friend of his because the apartment lady said, "No rabbits sir." My Dad said Chunk was happy at his new house because he had his own bedroom. I think I should ask him how he managed to get his own room. He might even have a telephone too. I don't think I want a telephone because I don't have a pocket. Now if I were a kangaroo . . . .

So, back to your question. You could try giving your Mom a nice stick from the backyard. If you bring it to her and she throws it away, it doesn't mean she thinks the stick is a bad present. It means she wants you to bring it back. It's a game they seem to like to play. I think it's called the "Throw a Stick Over and Over and Make your Pup Bring it Back" game. It will make you tired but it will probably make her happy in her heart.

Love,
Dr. Layla

Dear Layla,

My name is Doc Hillary. I am almost 9 months old, I have blonde curly hair and I love my mom and dad more than anything! I live in East Nashville where my mom loves to take me on walks near Shelby Park and my dad loves to throw the tennis ball in our awesome yard. I am writing to you Layla because I have a few questions that I don't think my parents know how to answer. Can you help?

First problem: My mom and dad leave me almost every morning a little after I wake up and eat. Where are they going and why don't they bring me with them?

Second problem: One of my favorite times of the day is when my mom comes home. I get so excited that I jump on her a lot. Is this bad? She sometimes doesn't like it, but I don't know how to stop. I just love seeing her!

Third problem: I love going to kickball with my mom and dad, and I watch from right near the bench. It is kind of muddy and I like to dig! Then when we get home my mom always puts me in the sink ... Why does she do that?

I hope you can help me Layla. I just want to be sure I am the best boy ever for my mom and dad, but I want to have fun too. Hope to play with you soon!

Love,
Doc

Doc
I am loved by Ryan and Jamie Lee

Hellos Doc Hillary!

<u>Problem 1</u>—*Sometimes my Mom and my Dad leave me on the UnLayla side of the door. It is not good when they say, "Sorry, you can't go." Those words makes me sad in my heart.*

Maybe you could try crying as loud as you can so they will feel bad about it and come back to get you. I don't think you should claw at the door though. My

Cousin Coco did that at Grammy's house and now she is going to have to paint it again to cover up all her little paw scratches. Grammy is going to have to paint it. I mean Grammy is painting the door. She is not painting Coco and Coco is not painting the door. That would be weird.

__Problem 2__—I am always glad to see my peoples, even if they have just been in another room. You are jumping because you are so happy. I don't know why peoples can't figure that out. I mean, when you are jumping up and down like a maniac, you are not doing it for no reason. That would be weird.

__Problem 3__—Oh poor Doc Hillary! The sink! They can't fool me! The sink is just a baby-sized version of the bathtub—The Bathtub Which Layla Hates. Moms have this thing about dirty pups.

I don't guess the reason for digging matters too much, it's the bath part that is the problem. Maybe you were bored. Sometimes we dig when we are bored. Maybe you just wanted to see if you could dig a hole deep enough to get to China. I might like to go to China. They have rice. I like rice. They have fortune cookies. I most definitely like cookies.

Next time you go to the kickball place and dig a hole, bring me back a cookie, OK?

Love,
Dr. Layla

Dearest Layla,

My little peoples whom I live with won't let me eat the yellow snow. They totally go bananas when I go near the yellow frozen stuff! Please help me understand. Can't a girl be free to eat what she wants?

Pups for life,
Phoebe

"Phoebe"
I am loved by Mallory, Sophie, and Isaac

Hellos Phoebe!

I am a little baffled at how to answer your question. It's fascinating that your peoples get really upset about Tinkle Pops. We had a big snow last year on my street and I didn't see any Tinkle Pops. Maybe next winter. I have heard other pups say they are quite delicious though.

Sometimes my peoples get torn up when I eat, drink, or chew on things they think are gross. Most pups have a highly developed sense of smell that makes many items of great interest to us. I mean, Baby Little Peoples put all kinds of things in their mouths—their fingers, shiny pennies, and even bugs, to name a few.

I saw a Baby Little People put its toes in its mouth and the mommy made a picture. When I chew on my toes, my mom say, "Stop it Layla!" Moms can be weird. I agree with you about the Tinkle Pops. I think I should like to try one if I ever get the chance.

Love,
Dr. Layla

Hi Layla,

My name is Chewy. I'm a boy. I live in Knoxville, Tennessee. I will be two years old on October 31st. I heard my peoples reading your stories and I hope you can help me.

When I get excited I can't help but jump up on my peoples to give them a hug. I sometimes forget that my paws are dirty and my peoples don't like to get dirty.

Some of my peoples are kind of short and when I hug them they fall over. How can I hug my peoples when I'm excited if they don't want me to?

Please help!
Chewy

"Chewy"
I am loved by Derek, Kay,
Griffin, Zoey, and Jonah

Dear Chewy,

Thank you for your letter. I'm sorry you get in trouble when you give Knock Down Hugs. Sometimes I give Knock Down Hugs to my peoples too. When I haven't seen my Mom or Dad for a while I do a huge

Knock Down Hug but they are not Little Peoples so I guess that helps them not to fall over.

You might want to try this—on your way towards them start screaming as loud as you can, "Hellos my people! I am heading in your direction to give you a Knock Down Hug! Brace yourself!" That will give them a chance to firmly plant their feet so by the time you get there they will be ready to receive your nice greeting.

Don't forget—be extra loud so they will hear you!

Love,
Dr. Layla

Dear Layla,

My name is Laynie Young. I live in Harvest, Alabama. I am 5 years old. I am a blonde long hair miniature dachshund or otherwise referred to as the most beautiful dog on the planet. Right now, I live with my mom, my MiMi, my Grumps, and my uncle Jason. Those are my people. The fur people that live with us are Bella, Kate, and Duke. They are all way bigger than me.

Here's my problem... Although I am the most beautiful dog on the planet, my breath is HORRIBLE. My MiMi says I can wake her up from a dead sleep if I yawn in the middle of the night. She calls it "howl-itosis." Me and my mom are about to get married and move in with my new daddy. Can you help me with my stinky situation? Thank you for any suggestions.

Love,
Laynie

"Laynie"
I am loved by Doug, Missy, Anna, and Jason

Hellos Laynie!

I can see from your picture you are a lovely girl. However, peoples just have a problem with stinky breath. When I was really little, my Mom would say, "Puppy breath is just so sweet." Now when I try to breathe in her face she says, "Layla, your breath is awful." She fans her face and it makes my breath blow away so she can't smell it anymore. That makes me sad in my heart.

My Mom and Dad get a plastic stick with white scratchies on it and rub it back and forth across my teeth. I think that is such a weird thing to do. I don't like it and I try to shut my mouth but my Mom rubs the plastic stick across my teeth anyway.

My cousin Maddie has to go to get her teeth brushed at a special place and they do it while she is asleep. I'm thinking it is because she might try to bite their finger instead of the plastic stick.

One time when she was there asleep they ripped out one of her teeth! It made me afraid to go to sleep for a while because I didn't want someone to rip out one of my teeth. I like all of my teeth and I want to keep them. I think that was mean to do while she was asleep because she could not say the words of, "Excuse me, but that tooth is mine and it is staying put peoples!"

I know Maddie would not have let that happen if she had been awake. Even though she is tiny, she is very brave. She chased the Package Man in the Big Brown Truck away from Grammy's house and he is as tall as a tree.

Ok. Back to you, Laynie. I guess you should probably let your mom rub the plastic stick with white scratchies across your teeth. You don't want to have to go to the special teeth brushing place and have a robber steal one of your pretty teeth like they did to Maddie!

As far as your breath problem goes, you may want to try some mints. Peoples eat them all the time before they mash their lips together. Evidently that breath thing must be a pretty big deal.

Try the plastic stick with white scratchie things. And mints, lots of mints. You can do this Laynie!

Love,
Dr. Layla

Dear Dr. Layla,

Hi! My name is Layla TOO! We must both have great Mommies to give us such a cool name. My question is, and you may not know either, when I am relaxing next to my Mama in the recliner at night sometimes I have tummy pains. Then a really bad smell shows up and my Mama scolds me. The smell that shows up is so bad I go to another seat and leave Mama with it. I walk away in disgust because I can't believe she would do such a vile thing!

I just don't understand why she gets on to me after she makes that horrible smell happen! I mean I just had a little tummy rumble. So do you know why Mommies are like that?

Most Sincerely,
Layla

Layla
I am loved by Anna

Hellos Other Layla!

I like your name very much because it makes the same sound as mine and that is a glad thing in my heart. And, yes, we both must have great Mommies for putting that name on us.

I can relate to your question. Next time you hear that rumble sound coming from your tummy you should probably go ahead a move so you can make a quick getaway before the putrid air escapes. If it follows you, you can move faster to out-run it.

You might not want to sit on your peoples when you feel a tumble rumble coming on. They might not like it if drop your air on them.

You can buy some spray to make the air smell better, I think. I'm not sure what happens to the bad air. The can might grab the bad air and stuff it inside. Who knows? Peoples seem to like those sprays a lot so I'm guessing that would solve your problem.

Love,
Dr. Layla

Hey, Layla!

My name is Max Beagle Bentley. I am a rescue pup of the Beagle breed. My mom got me at the shelter about 7 years ago. I am probably about 8 years old now, but I don't know my birthday.

I have two questions. First, every so often, my Mom puts me into the van. This is not a good thing because if we get in the van we go to a very bad place. It's called "The Vet" and "The Vet" is a bad, bad, bad man! He gives me "shots" which means he sticks things in my skin. I cry, but my mom says, "It is okay, Max." I try to show her my sad eyes and tell her it is NOT okay, but she doesn't understand.

Then, when I think it could not be any worse, another person that is dressed like "THE VET" comes in with a very, very, very long stick. Layla, I don't want to embarrass you, but this stick is VERY long and I am VERY small...and the stick goes...where NO stick should ever go! I do not like the stick. I cry more.

Mommy pets me and says, "It is okay, Max." This is most positively NOT OKAY! How do I tell Mommy this is not natural? How do I tell Mommy that "The VET" is an evil man! I think all pups should unite! We should find all people who are "The Vet" and bite them!

The second question is about what happens after I go to the very bad place and see "The Vet." Mommy drives by a place she calls "Arby's" on the way home. She rolls down the clear see-out part of the van and I can hear someone say, "Welcome to Arby's! How can I help you today?" Mommy orders what she calls an "Arby's Beef N Cheddar" for me as a treat after my horrible, very bad day.

Sometimes I am still so sad from "The Vet" that I can't enjoy the Heavenly thing she gets for me as a treat! We drive just a few more pupsteps and the lady inside the building hands mommy the treat. Mommy opens it right there! It is warm and smells of all kinds of good people food! So, Layla...how can I tell Mommy this very, very important message: "NO MORE VET...LOTS MORE ARBY's"

Love,
Max

"Max"
I am loved by Gwen

Hellos Max!

Although I know all about "The Place" you are talking about, I think I should turn this question over to a friend who is more qualified than I am to give you an answer. Let me introduce you to my friend, Sheldon. The rest of the letter is from him. It is from Sheldon. Not from me, Layla. OK?

Hi Max! I'm Sheldon, or Sir Sheldon as my doctor lady likes to call me. I am 5 years young. I'm writing to tell you about my doctor lady in case any other friends need to go to the special place that looks really scary. My mommy calls it the vet.

My heart was working too hard and it was making me tired. I was coughing and didn't feel like playing. My mommy carried me to the special place that looks really scary. I even had to stay overnight!!! I didn't get to sleep with my mommy so I was really sad. I thought maybe I had to stay at the special place that looks really scary

forever and wouldn't get to see my mommy. But Dr.

Dixon, my doctor lady, kept telling me it was okay. She said she was going to fix my heart and then I could go home with mommy.

Dr. Dixon had lots of special helpers that rubbed my belly and gave me treats! She put some cold gooey stuff on me and then I could see my heart on her mini television screen. She gave me some magic juice that made me really sleepy. When I woke up Dr. Dixon said she was all done! She said my heart was as good as new and I could see my mommy very soon!

The next day mommy came to get me and I was so happy in my heart! I don't cough anymore and I have lots of energy to run and play! So, if any pet friends hear their mommy or daddy say they have to go to the special place that looks really scary, it's okay! Don't be afraid. The doctor ladies and misters will just help you feel better and then give you treats!

Love
Dr. Layla, assisted by Sir Sheldon

Sheldon
I am loved by Ashley

Howdy, Layla!

My name is Julian and I am a rescued pup. I came from the shelter in August 2006. I was only about 3 months old then. I am a boy, but no one knows what kind of pup I am. The vet--who is a wicked, evil man-- says I am probably part Boxer and part Mountain Cur. My Gramma Gwen says I am "The best dog, ever!"

One question I have is: WHY do my people laugh when I turn upside down and wiggle to scratch my back? My people think it's so funny. Don't they have to wiggle and scratch, too?

My peoples have a farm--a turtle farm. It's the craziest thing a pup ever heard of! It's nice to get to swim in the ponds, but those turtles bite! I have tried to make friends with some of them and they do not like to be friends with doggies! I want my peoples to get rid of turtles and have a HAPPY DOGGY FARM!

How do I tell them my idea? Also...do you know anyone who would want to buy all the turtles? Maybe I could sell them the next time my peoples go on vacation! Then, they wouldn't have to work with turtles and they could just enjoy giving me treats!

Love,
Julian

"Julian"
I am loved by Hunter

Hellos Julian!

My peoples laugh when I do synchronized swimming on the rug to scratch my itchy back. My Mom has a sisal rug, which is a scruffy kind of plant used to make all kinds of things. Anyway, it feels wonderful on my back and I do lots of wild looking tricks trying to reach my itch.

Right after I get out of The Bathtub that Layla Hates I always cry until my Mom lets me go outside. Then I go roll in the grass to rub all the clean off of me. My Mom says that is not a good idea but I think it is very smart.

I think I would like to come see you one day on the turtle farm. I'm curious about how you grow them. Where can you buy turtle seeds? I'm going to tell my Dad to buy me some because I would like to plant turtle seeds and grow my own turtle.

Love,
Dr. Layla

Dear Layla,

I am a rescued pup so I don't know my birthday. I live on a farm and get to play outside all the time. When I first came to live with my daddy, I was so small, I slept in his shoe. It was snuggly and smelled like my daddy. Now, it doesn't fit so well. Can you tell me how to make my daddy's shoe big enough to sleep in, again?

Also, when Gramma Gwen is working outside, she puts something on her skin that smells good. She says it keeps the bugs from biting. I don't know about that, but I like to lick it off her legs. Gramma doesn't like that.

Can you tell me how to make her understand that I like to lick the sweet-smelling stuff? And besides...it's free kisses from her Grandpup! Why doesn't Gramma like that?

I'm sending you of picture of me from when I was first pup-adopted and I was sleeping in my Daddy's shoe.

Love,
Ryder

"Ryder"
I am loved by Hunter and Dakota

Hellos Ryder!

I'm not very sure about how to make a shoe bigger. Maybe you could put all of your daddy's shoes in a pile like in your picture and lay on top of them. It might not feel very soft and comfy but it would have his nice smell on them so that should make up for it.

I like how my Dad smells too. He's a good Dad. My Mom says I am a Daddy's Girl. One time when he was gone on a trip I got in trouble with my Mom. My Mom said the words to me of, "That was not a good thing to do, Layla." I laid in front of the door until he got home. I was going to tell on her. I gave her the stink eye until my Dad got back.

Love,
Dr. Layla

Dear Beautiful Layla,

My name is Bear—after the great Alabama Football coach, Bear Bryant. My mommy is an Alabama Football fan so she says "ROLL TIDE" a lot during what she calls football season. I am a male "rescued pup." I am half lab and half shepherd. I don't know my birthday, but I am about 2 years old. My mommy brings me treats all the time so most every day seems like my birthday!

Here is my question for you, beautiful Layla: There is something my Mommy says to me that I do not understand. She usually says this thing to me when I have been a little bad. The last time I sneaked and ate the rest of the bag of treats, Mommy laughed and said to me, "Bear, you are in trouble and I should spank your furry bottom!" Mommy is always smiling when she says this to me. She tells me how handsome I am, too! So, my question, Layla is, what is a spanking? Is it a good thing? I can't see my furry bottom so I don't know if Mom has given me a spanking on it or not.

Love,
Bear

P.S. You should come to visit me and we can play!

"Bear"
I am loved by Gwen

Hellos Bear!

My Daddy and Mommy say "Roll Tide" too even though we live in Tennessee! My G would like your name because he used to watch that Bear Football Man when he was a little boy.

Your furry bottom is the part of you that is on the back-ish side. I'm whispering this part because it is embarrassing, "It's close to where your doodles fall out."

My Mommy tells me she is going to spank me too. But mostly she just says the words of "Layla Jane!" Then I know I am in trouble. But, if she says, "Layla

Jane Skipworth" I run like a bullet away from her! My Mom does not hit me so I'm not scared of her. I'm just scared of the "Layla Jane Skipworth" sound because her voice gets hard and I know she is not a happy Mommy.

My Dad points at me and his voice gets bigger than usual. I crumple down like he has broken my heart into tiny little pieces. He feels bad and then it's all OK. Parents. You've just got to know how to work them.

Next time your Mom says she's going to spank your furry bottom, you can hide it really quick by sitting on it. When you sit on your bottom, it disappears. You know she's not ever going to spank it but, just in case, I would hide it anyway.

Love,
Dr. Layla

Hi Layla,

My name is Rajah and I am a fur-boy. I live in Florence, Alabama with my Mommy. My birthday is August 23 and I just turned 3. Here's my question: Why does mom want me to walk soooo slow and be sooo quiet? She takes me to the park and wants me to walk beside her but I think we both need exercise so I pull hard and walk fast! And of course I bark loudly to tell strangers to stay away from me and mom but she thinks I'm being impolite! What do you think?

Thanks,
Rajah

"Rajah"
I am loved by Ashley

Hellos Rajah!

When I am trying to get somewhere really fast and my Mom or Dad is holding my harness I make gaggedy sounds. I have to say to myself, "Slow down Layla because this is not a good idea." One time when I saw G at the bottom of the steps, I almost pulled Grammy down. I did the gaggedy thing and reminded myself I should slow myself a little.

I don't like when people talk to my Mom if I've never smelled them before. If I smell them and I don't like the way they come in my nose then I holler really loud, *"Don't get close to me or to my Mom!"* My Mom says I am being rude but I don't think she understands the smell good principle.

One time when I was at my Nana and Pa's house I rolled in some dead fish and my dad made gaggedy sounds. It was not a happy day for me because I had to take TWO baths! Two baths in one day is not a good thing!

So, don't roll in dead fish before you meet people. I'm thinking that will not make a good impression.

If they insist on saying words to your mom, you can always sit quietly but still give them the stink eye. Don't make a growly sound in your throat though because you don't want them to think you are mean. I'm sure the stink eye will make your point.

Love,
Dr. Layla

Dear Layla,

Hi! My name is Bell Wheat. I am 9 years old and I am a party colored Papillon or butterfly dog. They call me that because of my fluffy ears, they look like butterfly wings! I live in what my human mom calls Roll Tide country otherwise known as Tuscaloosa, Alabama!

Here are my questions. I'm sorry I have three. I hope that's OK. My human mom yells at the box with the pictures that move. When the humans in matching clothes are running around on that beautiful green grass she says "Roll Tide" a lot and seems happy. I just don't get it! She likes it when I run in our grass but she never says "Roll Tide" to me!

The next thing I need to know is, why does my mom ask me questions and then laugh at my answers?

Lastly, how can I get her to give me more treats? Thanks for your help!

Your paw pal,
Bell

"Bell"
I am loved by Le'Anne

Dear Bell,

My Uncle Hero Tommy yells at the picture box too! All the Teenage Middle People in my family watch him to see how long he can wait before he throws his hat on the ground and says, "Good grief!" or "Pitiful!" His voice gets big and his face gets a little reddish too sometimes.

I guess your mom likes for you to run on the grass outside since you can't get inside the picture box. It would be awful if you got stuck in there and couldn't get out. Besides, my picture box is flat and it would make my insides squish out if I tried to squeeze into it. That just made me shiver a little.

My Mom and Dad ask me stuff all the time too. I tilt my head and stare at them hoping it will help me understand what they are saying. Then they ask me again and I tilt my head the other way. They laugh and laugh because they keep asking and I keep tilting. Sometimes moms and dads are just weird that way.

As far as your final question, I think you should not ask about any extra treats. Just go ahead and take them. It would be OK if you did because they are your treats anyway. I've never seen my Mom or Dad fix themselves a bowl of my treats, so I think it is safe to assume they are all for me. Your mom probably feels the same way. Since they are yours, help yourself.

Love.
Dr. Layla

Dear Layla,

Layla, this is your cousin, McLovin, writing this letter. I have a question for you. Sometimes when we have a lot of people over I get nervous and depressed so I want my mom to put me in my kennel. Why do I feel that way? I love my peoples very much and I love you Layla. Can you help me, please?

Signed,
McLovin

"McLovin"
I am loved by Brad, Melissa, and Martha

Hellos McLovin!

You are awfully smallish and some visitors can be really big. That is probably a scary thing for a little guy like you. Don't be sad though. Look at it this way, it makes your peoples happy to have visitors. You want your peoples to be happy so you will have to keep letting peoples come over.

Pretend your kennel is a sailboat or a rocket ship. It will make you feel like you are having an adventure. I think that might be a good thing for you to try.

Love,
Dr. Layla

Hellos, Layla!

My name is Lucy. I am your Instagram pal. I am 9 years old--we thinks. I was rescued and they thought I was about six. We celebrate June 23rd as my birthday and Gotcha Day! Running out of toes to hold up! I am a fur-girl and I live in Saranac Lake, New York with my mom and my dad.

My question for you is...what would you think about your mom and dad getting you a little brother or sister some day? Would you be happy to have a playmate?

Love,
Lucy

P.S. Mom started reading your diary last night :) She loves it!

Lucy
I am loved by Britt and Andy

Hellos Lucy!

I don't know if I would like a fur sibling. There's only one of me at my house and I am just a little spoiled—says my Mom. I don't have to share my toys, my treats, or my food. And, more importantly, I don't have to share my Mom or Dad. I'm thinking I would not like that very much.

My G is always asking my Mom and Dad to give him a Baby Little People. Grammy tells him to stop asking because she says it has to be their decision. G doesn't care. He keeps asking.

I think I should like to have a Baby Little People at my house. They usually smell like milk and some kind of biscuit I can't quite identify. I like that smell very much.

Sometimes Baby Little Peoples don't have the milk smell. They smell like a doodle. They don't drop their doodles on the floor though. They wear their doodles in a little bag strapped to their bottom. Sometimes they cry until someone changes their doodle bag. Sometimes they wear their doodle bag for a while until someone gets a whiff and they make a funny face.

Since doodles are a part of life, I could learn to live with it, I suppose. I think I would very much like for my Mom and Dad to have a Baby Little People to add to our house. I like the way they smell, most of the time.

Love,
Dr. Layla

Dear Layla:

I am an 8 year old boy named, hmmm, uhm, Anonymous. I've just been wondering about a problem I have and I thought you would know what to do about it. I want to make sure I look great for my parents.

Sometimes after I'm done grooming I get a nasty cough. After a while it gets worse and I hack up a weird misshapen wad that just looks awful. I guess I need to find a way to stop this habit. Please reply.

Signed,
Anonymous

Anonymous—Aka "Chip"
I am loved by Jake and Aaron

Hellos Anonymous!

I must admit I am stumped by your question. It actually sounds like you might have a serious medical issue. It is terrifying to even say this but I think it is quite possible that you may be coughing up a hairball. That is a very odd thing to happen to you because it is more like something that would happen to a cat. Hey! Wait a minute! Is that you Chip? Chip, you ARE a cat!

This is a book for pups like me! Chip, I am refusing to answer your question. Someone else will have to help you with your gross situation. I'm outta here!

From,
Dr. Layla

Dear Layla,

My name is Milo! I am three toes old, but in November I will be four toes old. I am a boy Standard Poodle and live in Huntsville, Alabama with my mommy and daddy.

We go on all kinds of adventures together. We especially love going to the park to play with the duckies and meet other puppies, but sometimes when we go out we see people that want to pet me it makes me a little scared. What is something I can do to be less scared?

Love,
Milo

"Milo"
I am loved by Zach and Amanda

Hellos Milo!

Peoples are always wanted to pet me too. Big Peoples. Little Peoples. Even Baby Little Peoples want to run their chubby hands onto my fur coat. Most of the time I don't mind, but some days, I just don't want any hands on me. I am especially not wanting any hands on me that I have not smelled before.

Some peoples who want to touch me don't even ask my Mom or Dad first! That is not a glad thing in my heart. I have to smell their peopleness and let my nose register whether their peopleness is good or bad. If they smell like food they usually get to pet me right then.

If I smell their peopleness and there is an aroma of another girl or boy like me, then I've got to decide if they are friend or foe before they get to pet me. That's a lot of brain work going on between my ears so they have got to give me a little time.

I think maybe you could try writing a sign and hanging it around your neck. The words would say, "Hellos. My name is Milo. Ask my Mom or Dad if you can pet me first. Give me the back of your hand so I can take a whiff. I'll need a minute to decide if you pass the test or not. Do. Not. Just. Pet. Me.

When you make your sign, write it with a crayon because crayons look friendly and you will have lots of colors to choose from. Personally, I like pink or purple but you might want something different. Green is nice. Grass is green. I like grass very much. Go with the green.
Love,
Dr. Layla

Dear Layla,

My name is Dutch, but sometimes mommy and daddy call me Dux. I am two years old. My birthday is March 14th.

I have a big fur sister named Kuma. Kuma has taught me everything I know about how to be a good pup. She has been my role model from the beginning. If I don't know where she is, I get scared and I go find her so I can be with her. In fact, ever since I was a little pup I've been kind of a scaredy cat. I would give anything to be braver like my sister Kuma!!

I want to sniff out tracks by myself. I want to have

the confidence to go explore something new that I've never seen and not be so scared. Layla, do you think you have any advice to help me be braver?
Love,
Dutch

P.S. Sometimes mommy and daddy give us yummy scraps and Kuma will eat all the bites before I can have any!!!! Can you believe that!?!?!?

"Dutch"
I am loved by Steven and Jessica

Hellos Dutch!

I'm sorry you called yourself a scaredy cat. If there is anything I do not want to be, it is anything associated with a cat! I can relate to your problem because there are some things I am scared of myself. I don't like thunderstorms, fireworks, or hats. One time, when I was a baby, my Mom had to dress up for work and she wore a hat. It scared me so bad I dropped a doodle out by accident! My Mom and Dad laughed but I was embarrassed.

You look like a very strong boy. Go over to the mirror every morning and say these words, "I am a brave boy. I am a brave boy. I am a brave boy." Then picture yourself doing something brave, like fighting a dragon.

Love,
Dr. Layla

PS: I'm sorry Kuma is quick to get to the treats. My Cousin Maddie does that to Cousin Coco all the time. Maddie may be elderly, but when it comes to treats, she is fast, fast, fast. I don't have to share my treats with anyone and I am glad about that thing.

Dear Layla,

My name is Kuma, and I am two years old. I will be turning the big three on September 17. I live the most happy life in Florence, Alabama with my mom, dad, and younger brother, Dutch. I am the Miss Alpha of our home and Dutch follows me around like I am a queen. I love it! Even though everything usually always goes my way, there's one problem I have and I hope you can help me with it. A lot of people come visit our house. I get all excited and do my sweet "rooooooo" sound when I introduce myself. Mom and Dad think it is so cute, but visitors don't!

Here's the thing—they don't get excited like I do. The people that come to my house are always scared of me. They think I'm going to hurt them. I have never hurt or bit anybody! My Mom or Dad have to put me outside in the back to keep me away from everybody so I miss out on petting and love. It makes my eyes rain. What can I do so people won't think I'm scary to look at?

Sincerely,
Kuma

"Kuma"
I am loved by Steven and Jessica

Hellos Kuma!

From your picture I can see you are quite a lovely lady so I can't imagine why anyone would ever be afraid of you. I am sorry that rain comes from your eyes when you are sad about being put outside. I don't like it when I have to be on the un-Layla side of the door either.

Maybe you could try looking humble when someone comes to your house. Hunch your shoulders a little and get low to the ground so you will look smaller.

Instead of making a "rooooooo" sound you could do a "bah . . . bah . . . bah . . ." like a sheep. Nobody is scared of sheep. See if that works for you.

Love,
Dr. Layla

PS: Can you please let your brother Dutch get some treats too? That would be a very nice thing for you to consider doing. He's a little sad about that situation.

Dear Dr. Layla,

Hello! I'm Sadie Hall. I'm 10 months old and I live in Center Star, Alabama and I'm a fur-girl.

I have a problem with floor tiles. They're so slippery! My peoples cross it with ease and want me to come on to it too, but I can't! I have to travel on the dining room rug. I cannot get into the kitchen with all those yummy smells! :(Please help!

Also, I don't understand it when my family gets mad because I grabbed some dirty socks, shorts, and other fun chewy cloth. I just want something to chew on! I've chewed up, I think, all of Jacob's baseballs. I keep losing my chew toys so I have to find a substitute. I chewed up all the pillows and my family took them away from me because they were tired of picking up stuffing.

Another question I have is, "What do you do when you want to be friends with a cat?" They are not all that different. Cats are just funny looking dogs. I want to be friends but the cat doesn't. My older best friend, Lacy, said that cats are terrible and they don't want friends. Is that true? I probably need to learn more about cats. Do they greet each other differently than dogs? Do you think that's the problem? Cats and dogs can get along. I just don't think the cat thinks that they can.

See, I'm a puppy so I don't understand a lot of things. Will you help? You are a wise, smart, and experienced dog.

Please help,
Sadie

"Sadie"
I am loved by Jacob and Anna Lee

Hellos Sadie!

As far as the slippery floor tiles go, I think you could try those little socks with the rubber grippers on the bottom. You would have to get two pairs though since you would need them for all four of your leggies. Maybe then you could get to the kitchen easier. I love the kitchen at Grammy's house. She drops things accidently on purpose for me all the time.

Peoples just don't understand why we need to chew

on things. Personally, I like tennis balls but that is because there are no baseballs at my house. If there were baseballs I'm thinking I would probably have to see if they were chewable too.

My peoples gave me a toy that was lots of fun. Then it got a hole in it and started snowing from the side. My Mom threw it away because it kept snowing all over the floor. Peoples are weird that way for some reason. When there is lots of snow outside they want to play in it. They make packed up wads of it and throw it at each other and laugh. Then, when my toy snowed from the side, my Mom threw it away. Silly peoples.

My sweet Sadie, there is a huge difference between dogs and cats. And I mean huge. They have sharp finger knives and you don't want to get near them! They may have a fur coat like us and walk on four leggies, but trust me on this one, they are NOT like us! At! All!

Cats make an awful whiny sound that goes "Meow. Meow." They rub their nastiness on peoples' legs and flick their tails all over them. They are conniving and sneaky. They drop their doodles in a box of rocks and then hide them like they are some kind of special treasure.

They think they are the best but they are truly the worst. Sadie, don't do it. Don't ever be friends with a cat. Seriously, don't. I mean it, Sadie. Don't do it.

Love,
Dr. Layla

Dear Dr. Layla,

Magnum here! I'm writing this for me and my brother, Jack. We live with our Mom and Dad. When I was a tiny pup, I was the last one left and my Dad rescued me from someone who was going to throw me away. I'm about 8 years old. Our Mom and Dad found Jack on the side of the road. Unless I'm counting wrong, I think he's about 7 years old.

We were hoping you could answer some questions for us. The thing is, we're kind of scaredy cats when it comes to thunder. We get so scared that we tear up the house trying to get inside to hide from the big scary noises coming from the sky. Our parents have tried to tell us it's just God rearranging furniture, but we can't help freaking out a little when we hear it. Do you have any advice for us chickens?

Love,
Magnum & Jack

"Jack and Magnum"
We are loved by Justin and Chelsea

Dear Magnum and Jack,

I am sorry to hear you are troubled by storms. I know there are little jackets you can wear that make you feel better when it flashes and booms outside. The last time I was at Grammy's the flash and boom started and I got close to my G. I felt all quivery in my insides, which made me quivery on my outsides.

Grammy got a nice soft towel from the bathroom and wrapped it around my middle. Then she wrapped a big bandage around the towel to make it fit me in a cozy way. I felt a little better. I still stayed close to G though because I really like that man. He has huge arm muscles so I think I'm pretty safe with him.

Make sure to stay inside when the flashing and booming starts. And, whatever you do, don't go out there with an umbrella because you might fly away. Especially Jack, since he is kind of smallish. No umbrellas for you, ok? Stay safe!

Love,
Dr. Layla

Dear Layla,

Our names are Gauge and Pepper. We live in Columbia, Tennessee. We are brothers and best friends. We are both in our late 50's, or 9 in human years. Being so mature, we thought we had our humans trained pretty good. This all changed a few months ago when they brought home this miniature human! She cried a LOT for the first few weeks she was in our home. She is getting better but she still wakes us up in the middle of the night. Mommy says it's cause she needs some milk or may have a wet bottom. When we are wet we just shake it off, so I don't know why that would be a big deal.

Mommy is probably just not good at that game the little girl likes to play that mommy calls "Guess what's wrong with Johanna!" Our mommy looks really tired when she is giving the mini human her milk when it is still dark outside.

She even gives the mini human her breakfast before we get OUR breakfast! Sometimes we lick her leg or arm to help her stay awake! How can we get our new little human to stay asleep till mommy and daddy wake us up to eat and go potty? We are too old to be losing out on so much rest every night. It is cutting in to our awake and play time during the day because we have to nap all the time! Please help Dr. Layla! Thanks in advance for any recommendations.

Your friends,
Gauge and Pepper

PS: Can we ask you one more question, please? We don't won't to be a bother, but we know this will be one of your areas of expertise! How come our parents let us lick their faces, but won't let us lick the baby human's face? The bottom of her face is always shining with what our mommy calls slobber! Our Mimi filled us in on a little secret about this slobber stuff! She says the baby human is so sweet that she is dripping with liquid sugar! Don't mom and dad know how much we like sugar? Why can't we have any of this slobber, we mean liquid sugar?

"Gage and Pepper"
We are loved by Ross, Stephanie, and Johanna

Hellos Gauge and Pepper!

I'm sorry the Tiny Baby Little People appeared at your house and took over. I'm also sorry it changed up your nice routine. Tiny Baby Little Peoples are just like that sometimes.

They often start with a smallish kind of cry but when they are wound up they keep making a squawk until someone gives them whatever they want. I should know. I do the same thing.

The Tiny Baby Little People may be new in the house but they sure know how to get their way. When they start that crying sound the Big Peoples keep trying all kinds of things to make them happy again.

Tiny Baby Little Peoples don't care if it is dark outside either. If they want to make that loud crying sound they do it. They don't care if everyone in the house wakes up. They don't even care if the whole neighborhood wakes up.

Sometimes after Tiny Baby Little Peoples have a bottle, they have to let their extra air out. It makes a loud "Burrrrrrrrp." I wonder how such a big sound can come from such a Tiny Baby Little People.

It is a really bad thing when their air gets trapped on the inside of them. They cry louder and louder until the air whooshes out of the lower end of them. Sometimes the peoples laugh at the air release sound. That is so weird to me. It's not funny at all. It is smart because there is more room on the outside of you than on the inside of you.

When the Tiny Baby Little People's doodle bag is wet, I guess it probably is uncomfortable. Especially when it fills up and gets really saggy. That's why I leave my tummy water outside in the grass.

I'm sorry the Tiny Baby Little people gets its breakfast first, ahead of you. Before it came to your house, you had a good thing going and now it's all different. But, pretty soon, the Tiny Baby Little People will stretch out into just a regular sized Little People. This is a good thing because it might throw the ball to you or pet your fur coat and tell you that you are handsome. When they say those words, it will make you happy in your heart.

Tiny Baby Little Peoples like to play the game of I'm

Up, Now Everyone is Up. There will not be any sleeping late for you until it becomes a Teenage Middle People. I'm sorry to inform you of that fact. But for now, anytime the Tiny Baby Little People is asleep, you better rest yourself because you never know when it will wake up and start that wailing sound.

Moms and dads don't like for you to give a Tiny Baby Little People kisses on their face. They don't mind if you take a whiff of them, but no kissing. I know it is tempting but it is not a good idea. You will get in trouble. Trust me on this one.

Love,
Dr. Layla

Hello Layla!

My name is Blaze and I am almost a year old. I am from Town Creek, Alabama. My feet are kind of big so I guess I will be growing a little more.

I need your help, pronto! We had a visitor at our house. He left his People Device sitting down low. I could not pass it up. I grabbed it and buried it under the dirts. When everyone was searching for it, I looked smug because I knew where I had hidden it. My Nana got her People Device and used it to make the other People Device beep. No more smug face for me because they dug up all the dirts and found it. I was in some serious trouble.

Here's my real problem. I have a brother named Bama. He's older than me. I understand that part, but I do not understand why he gets all this special treatment. Bama gets to ride in the golf cart and I have to run beside it trying to keep up. So, when no one was looking, I chewed up the steering wheel. If I can't ride, I'll fix it where no one gets to ride.

Later on, I looked inside the glass door and there was Bama, inside! In the air-conditioned inside! So, I chewed up the porch steps that lead to the door. If I can't go inside in the air-conditioning, no one is going to be able to go inside in the air-conditioning. How can I get my parents to give me some special treatment?

Love,
Blaze

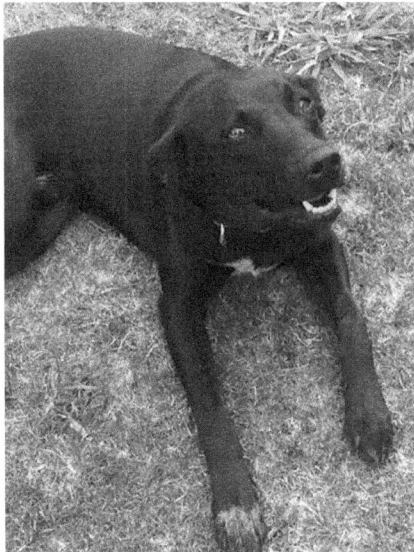

"Blaze"
I am loved by Blaire, Bryce, and Baylor

Hellos Blaze!

I'm sorry to hear that your brother, Bama, gets extra loves. I kind of have it made at my house. I'm the only one of me so I don't have to share anything at all. I like that part very much.

I have been giving your problem careful consideration. I think I have a wonderful solution. You need to make your own set of keys for the golf cart. Then you could drive yourself around while Bama and all your peoples chase after you!

If that doesn't get you some extra attention you could lock all your peoples outside and then you can sit on the couch under the air-conditioning. That should make your family notice you.

Love,
Dr. Layla

Dear Layla,

My name is HHollis. Yes, my name starts with two H's which means I was born at Lackland Air Force Base in San Antonio, Texas. They give us names with a double first letter as identification. They name each litter of puppies alphabetically throughout the year, just like weathermen name hurricanes!

Lackland Air Force Base is where the US Military raises future Military Working Dogs, mainly Belgian Malinois like me. Even though I am a Belgian Malinois people always call me a German Shepherd . . . can you believe that?

After I was born, I lived with my daddy and

mommy for 7 months, then I went to camp to learn to be a working dog. It was very hard, and I missed my family. After 2 months, I decided I did not want to be a military dog after all, so I went back home for good. Now, I am one year old. I live with my daddy, mommy, and older fur-sister, Laddy, in Colorado Springs, Colorado.

Here's my problem......I'm not going to name names but let's just say one of my parents likes my older fur sister, Laddy, better than me. I mean I'm cuter, smaller, and the BEST cuddler! Can you help me with my problem?

Love,
HHollis

"HHollis"
I am loved by Jackson and Beth

Hellos HHollis,

There's a lot of that "special treatment" going around. I think you need to do some things to get attention. Try limping around a little like you have something stuck in your paw. Surely that will get you some sympathy. Your Mom and Dad will try to figure out what is wrong and give you some bonus petting.

I may have an even better suggestion. Don't eat. I know it will be hard but that just tears peoples up— especially Mom Peoples. She will be so worried about you that she will give you extra loves. She might even promise to give you a treat if you will eat your food!

Sometimes I don't eat my food and I hold out on my hunger strike until my Mom sprinkles a little cheddar cheese on top of my kibbles. Then I gobble it up. That should take care of the Mom Peoples part.

When your dad comes home, jump up in his lap. Look right into his face and let your eyes get a little waterish. He will feel bad and give you extra loves then too. Try these solutions HHollis. I'm sure they will work for you!

Love,
Dr. Layla

Hellos Layla!

I was at the park next to the library with my People Mom and I saw a book with the most beautimus dog I had ever never saw. My mom said it was you and your name is Layla and yous have a book.

My name is Bentley and I'm a blue dog! Well...wait...I'm not a blue dog. I'm a boy dog who has a blue blanket in my crate. You know when your People Mom and People Dad brings home one of those new Tiny Peoples and they have a pink blanket or a blue blanket in their crate and it means they are a boy or a girl People Person? I am a boy.

But I'm not a People boy I'm a fur boy! My mom calls me her fur boy. When I do something not wrong then I'm a "good fur boy!" I am five toes old. I tries to show my friends but they can't see my toes cause they are all covered with fur! So I just barks five times when they asks me how old I am.

I live with my People Mom and People Dad in a place with a funny name that is called Killen, Alabama. I live on a big green pasture with a creek! And my favoritest thing in the whole world is to swim in the creek! Do you likes to swim? Swimming is my fur hobby!

I love it when my fur gets all wet and I run and run to see how long it takes for me to dry it! It's like a People Person using one of those long things that blows hot air and they bend their head over and wave it around and it dries their People fur! I thinks that is crazy! I think it would be much much better if they would run around in circles and get it dry like me! Why don't they want to dry themselves like I do? I got to go now and lick the fountain! You would love the fountain because it has water that shoots out of a hard funny shaped rock! I would so so so much like to meet you one day Layla.

Bark to you later my new fur friend,
Bentley

"Bentley"
I am loved by David, Sherri, Cortney.
Adam, Seth, Taylor, and Erin

Hellos Bentley,

I do not understand why anyone would want to use one of those air blowers on their hairs. They are loud and whoosh out big puffs of air. I am not a fan of loud whooshing things.

Most peoples don't have pretty fur coats like us, so I guess they dry off really quick. Except for one man I saw that had some weird hairs growing from his ears and his nose. He would have to run really fast and hold his head back so the air could get to it to dry them.

I would very much like to visit you and drink water from your fountain. It all sounds so wonderful. Thanks for the invite.

Love,
Dr. Layla

Dear Dr. Layla,

Hi! It's me, your favorite cousin, Coco. I have been getting into a lot of trouble lately and I was hoping you could help me out. When my Mommy and Daddy leave, it's the only time the bin of mixed up treats are left unattended. There may be mashed potatoes, brownies, chicken wings and popcorn at the same time, so you can only imagine my dilemma!

I've learned a way to paw at it until it falls and spills its yummy cornucopia on the floor. I very much enjoy the feast that pours out each time. When my Mommy and Daddy come home, their voices get very loud and they always say, "BAD GIRL, COCO!" They leave it out for me every day, so I don't understand why they get mad when I get into it. Can you help me solve this mystery? I just don't understand!

Love,
Confused Cousin Coco

"Coco"
I am loved by Matt and Sarah

Hellos Coco!

I'm wondering why parents leave those snack containers out then say, "No! No! No!" If I ever try it, my Mom's voice gets big too and she says the words of, "Layla, that is dirty." I tell her it is not dirty. It has a nice white bag inside. It is full of wonderful goodness! She doesn't care.

No one should blame you for having a snack. When my Mom says the words of, "Layla that's dirty." I'm a little perplexed. I mean, think about it, it was just on her plate five minutes ago and now it's gross? If it was good enough for them to eat a few minutes earlier, what is wrong with me having a sample of it now? I know. Weird, right? Besides, it's a shame to let those lovely snacks go to waste.

I'm thinking you should get some beautiful stickers and decorate the outside of the container. Flower stickers might be nice. Maybe if it looked more pretty then your mom would be able to ignore the smell. Sometimes when G closes the white bag he makes a gaggedy sound. So does my Dad. The aroma doesn't bother me at all. I actually like it very much.

If the flower stickers don't make them forget the scent, then stand by the container and bark until they give in and knock it over for you. That way it will be their fault and not yours. You could not possibly be in trouble if your mom or dad does it. Try that!

Love,
Dr. Layla

Dear Dr. Cousin Layla,

Hi, Layla, this is Maddie speaking. I know we have been cousins for a long time, but for the benefit of your readers, I would like to share some information about myself. I came to live with my mom, Sarah, when I was one year old. I am now almost 11! When she married Matt, he adopted me, and became my dad.

My name is Madison, but I go by Maddie. I live with my parents and my sister, Coco, in Florence, Alabama. My Grammy, who, by the way, is your Grammy too, says that I remind her of a cranky old lady.

Now, on to my important question. I have an extremely embarrassing problem. Although I'm a very clean pup, but my Mom gave me the nickname, "Corn Chip Maddie." She says my paws smell like Fritos! How rude! I think I smell like sunshine and roses, but my family says otherwise. Is there anything that I can do to rid myself of this revolting development? My family would be forever grateful.

Sincerely,
Funky in Florence
Your Cousin Maddie

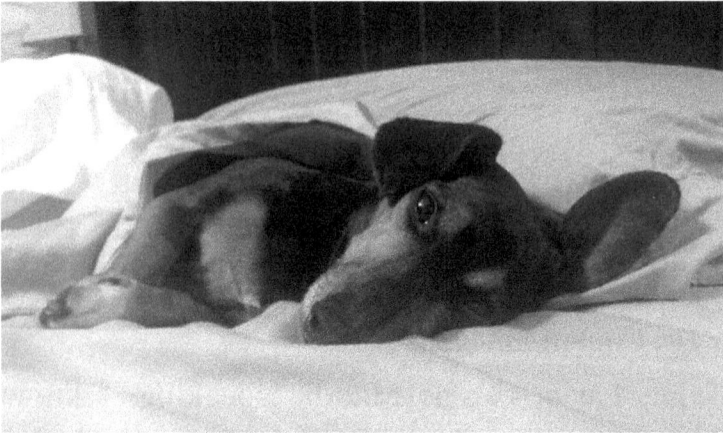

"Maddie"
I am loved by Matt and Sarah

Dearest Cousin Maddie,

I am sorry that Aunt Sarah and Uncle Matt have called you a name that makes you sad. However, I like corn chips very much so maybe you should look at it more as a compliment.

What you are suffering from is sometimes called "Frito Feet." There's a tiny little bug, so tiny you can't even see it. It is very sneaky because it hides on the bottom of your feet. The bug is what smells bad, not you, my sweet Maddie.

As long as your feet don't hurt you at all and there are no boo boos on them, it is not a problem for you. Everyone else will just have to deal with it. It may work to your advantage. When someone tries to get your spot on the couch, just stretch out and put your feet in their face. Unless they like corn chips a lot, they will either have to move on or keep smelling them.

Love,
Dr. Layla

Dear Dr. Layla,

My name is Emma Lou Phillips, but you can call me Emma. I'm just a simple country girl from Walnut Grove, Tennessee. I am 1 year old and my birthday is October 31st, on Halloween!

I love my parents SO much, but I have this problem. There is this really cool place next to my house; my parents call it a pasture, or something like that. Anyways, there are these creatures in the pasture that are much bigger than me and they make this weird sound that goes like this, "MOOOOOO!" Whatever that means! In the field where these creatures live, there are these piles of brown, mushy stuff that smell so wonderful and I just can't help but play in them! It's so much fun to just roll round in these mysterious, smelly piles. When I go home after playing, my parents get really upset with me. They get these mad voices and say things like "Bad girl" and "You stink." Then they give me a bath to wash off the brown stuff! I just don't know what to do! I don't like my parents being upset with me, but those piles are so tempting I just can't help myself! What should I do, Dr. Layla?

Your confounded fur-buddy,
Emma

"Emma"
I am loved by Rocky and Chelsea

Hellos Emma!

I like your birthday because it is Candy Day and any day with candy is a happy day for me. I also think your paws are just lovely. They are very pretty because they are polka dotted. Polka dots look happy. I like them very much.

Those creatures are called cows. That's where we get milk. And ice cream. I love ice cream! The mysterious piles near your house are actually the cows' doodles. And they are huge! I think if I left a doodle that big in my house my Dad might faint.

I guess your mom and dad get mad because they don't realize you just want to share your treasures with them. Haven't you ever heard one of the peoples say to another peoples, "You sure smell good?"

Don't your mom and dad know you are just putting on a little perfume for them? You could name it "Cow Pattie Delight" or "Au De Poopoo from the Pasture."

When my Grammy was a little girl she went with her cousins and her granddaddy to their Aunt Bertha's farm in the country. Grammy's cousin, Douglas, gave one of the big brown cow doodles a kick with his boot. The top was brown, but the inside was green! How interesting is that? She said Granddaddy made him put his boots in the trunk on the ride home. Sometimes peoples are just so weird.

Next time they give you a bath, just go straight outside afterwards and wallow all in the biggest cow doodle you can find. I think if you keep doing it enough times they will eventually get used to it and they will give up on the baths. That is—until your fur gets crunchy. If your fur gets crunchy that might be a little bit uncomfortable and you might even be glad to take a bath in that case.

Here's another option: Get your mom's perfume bottle and empty it all out in the sink. Then go get some of the cow doodles and mix it with a little water and pour it into the perfume bottle. That way, the next time your mom puts on perfume she will smell wonderful for you. I'm sure she will realize you are just trying to be sweet and she will appreciate all your efforts.

Love,
Dr. Layla

Hello Layla!

My name is B. That's right...just the letter B. I am the oldest of all my fur-friends and will be 8 toes next year on April 28th. We live in Florence, Alabama with my dad, Hey-Taylor, and my mom, Babe.

See Layla, the thing about my fur-friends is Hey-Taylor and Babe got them for me so I wouldn't be sad when they are gone to work. Even with my new friends I am still sad to see them leave. Truthfully, I would rather had been given ANYTHING else instead of these guys, maybe even a bath. With all these new dogs in the house Hey-Taylor and Babe have to play with them now too instead of just me.

My question for you Layla is, how do I take these friends back to where they came from and swap them for some toys and bones so my peoples can play with me more? Thank you for your help Layla.

Paws truly,
B

"B"
I am loved by Taylor and Ann

Hellos B!

I can see that you are the little guy of the group. As a matter of fact it looks as if you might be about to topple off the side of the bed. I think if you try to swap them for toys your peoples might notice since they are a kind of biggish.

Maybe you could just explain to them, in an ever so nice way, that you want them to find some new peoples to live with since your peoples were your peoples first. I mean, it is a reasonable request. You were there before them.

You may need to try to be a little more obvious. You can buy them all their own suitcases. If they don't get the hint, you may have to up your game. Since they are giants compared to you, nothing personal B, you've got to use your smarts.

You could pack a few things in their suitcases that they could take with them as souvenirs. Be sure to give them a picture of your peoples. They could look at the picture of them if they wanted to remember what your peoples look like in their faces.

You could include some of your peoples' clothes so they could smell them from time to time. But just make sure it is not one of your dad's work-out shirts because that would be gross.

Once you have their suitcases ready, set them out on the porch. Tell the other pups someone is at the door that wants to give them a treat. When they go outside, shut the door fast and lock it. Do not let them back in even if they cry.

Wow. I've just decided those words sound a little mean. If you locked them outside that would make them sad in their hearts so forget everything I just told you. You may actually be stuck with all those big guys.

Think about it and remember you were there first and your mom and dad have loved you longer. So really, you are the big winner even though you are kind of smallish.

Love,
Dr. Layla

www.ingramcontent.com/pod-product-compliance
Lightning Source LLC
Chambersburg PA
CBHW060656030426
42337CB00017B/2640